LAND TO LIGHT ON

LAND TO LIGHT ON

DIONNE BRAND

M&S

Canadian Cataloguing in Publication Data

Brand, Dionne, 1953–
    Land to light on

Poems.
ISBN 0-7710-1645-X

I. Title.

PS8553.R275L36 1997   C811'.54   C96-932345-X
PR9199.3.B72L36 1997

The publishers acknowledge the support of the Canada Council and the
Ontario Arts Council for their publishing program.

Typesetting by M&S, Toronto
Printed and bound in Canada

McClelland & Stewart Inc.
The Canadian Publishers
481 University Avenue
Toronto, Ontario
M5G 2E9

  2   3   4   5   01   00   99   98   97

to my sisters, born and found

CONTENTS

I HAVE BEEN LOSING ROADS

I i

Out here I am like someone without a sheet
without a branch but not even safe as the sea,
without the relief of the sky or good graces of a door.
If I am peaceful in this discomfort, is not peace,
is getting used to harm. Is giving up, or misplacing
surfaces, the seam in grain, so standing
in a doorway I cannot summon up the yard,
familiar broken chair or rag of cloth on a blowing line,
I cannot smell smoke, something burning in a pit,
or gather air from far off or hear anyone calling.
The doorway cannot bell a sound, cannot repeat
what is outside. My eyes is not a mirror.

I ii

If you come out and you see nothing recognisable,
if the stars stark and brazen like glass,
already done decide you cannot read them.
If the trees don't flower and colour refuse to limn
when a white man in a red truck on a rural road
jumps out at you, screaming his exact hatred
of the world, his faith extravagant and earnest
and he threatens, something about your cunt,
you do not recover, you think of Malcolm
on this snow drifted road, you think,
"Is really so evil they is then
that one of them in a red truck can split your heart
open, crush a day in fog?"

I iii

I lift my head in the cold and I get confuse.
It quiet here when is night, and is only me
and the quiet. I try to say a word but it fall. Fall
like the stony air. I stand up there but nothing
happen, just a bank of air like a wall. I could swear
my face was touching stone. I stand up but
nothing happen, nothing happen or I shouldn't say
nothing. I was embarrassed, standing like a fool,
the pine burdened in snow, the air fresh, fresh
and foreign and the sky so black and wide I did not
know which way to turn except to try again, to find
some word that could be heard by the something
waiting. My mouth could not find a language.
I find myself instead, useless as that. I sorry.
I stop by the mailbox and I give up.

I iv

I look at that road a long time.
It seem to close.
Yes, is here I reach
framed and frozen on a shivered
country road instead of where I thought
I'd be in the blood
red flame of a revolution.
I couldn't be farther away.
And none of these thoughts
disturb the stars or the pine
or the road or the red truck
screeching cunt along it.

I v

All I could do was turn and go back to the house
and the door that I can't see out of.
My life was supposed to be wider, not so forlorn
and not standing out in this north country bled
like maple. I did not want to write poems
about stacking cords of wood, as if the world
is that simple, that quiet is not simple or content
but finally cornered and killed. I still need the revolution
bright as the blaze of the wood stove in the window
when I shut the light and mount the stairs to bed.

II i

Out here, you can smell indifference driving
along, the harsh harsh happiness of winter
roads, all these roads heading nowhere, all
these roads heading their own unknowing way,
all these roads into smoke, and hoarfrost, friezed
and scrambling off in drifts, where is this
that they must go anytime, now, soon, immediately
and gasping and ending and opening in snow dust.
Quiet, quiet, earfuls, brittle, brittle ribs of ice
and the road heaving under and the day lighting up,
going on any way.

II ii

I have to think again what it means that I am here,
what it means that this, harsh as it is and without
a name, can swallow me up. I have to think how I
am here, so eaten up and frayed, a life that I was
supposed to finish by making something of it
not regularly made, where I am not this woman
fastened to this ugly and disappointing world.
I wanted it for me, to burst my brain and leap a distance
and all I have are these hoarse words that still owe
this life and all I'll be is tied to this century and waiting
without a knife or courage and still these same words
strapped to my back

II iii

I know as this thing happens, a woman
sucks her teeth, walks into a shop on an island
over there to stretch a few pennies across another
day, brushes a hand over her forehead and leaves,
going into the street empty-handed. Her certainty
frighten me. "Is so things is," she muse, reading
the shopkeeper's guiltless eyes, this hot hope the skin
tames to brooding, that particular advice, don't expect
nothing good. Quite here you reach and you forget.

no wonder I could get lost here, no wonder
in this set of trees I lose my way, counting
on living long and not noticing a closing,
no wonder a red truck could surprise me
and every night shape me into a crouch
with the telephone close by and the doors
checked and checked, all night. I can hear
everything and I can hear birds waking up
by four a.m. and the hours between three
and five last a whole day. I can hear wood
breathe and stars crackle on the galvanised
steel, I can hear smoke turn solid and this
house is only as safe as flesh. I can hear the
gate slam, I can hear wasps in my doorway,
and foraging mice, there's an old tree next
to my car and I can hear it fall, I can hear
the road sigh and the trees shift. I can
hear them far away from this house late, late
waiting for what this country is to happen,
I listen for the crunch of a car on ice or gravel,
the crush of boots and something coming

II v

A comet, slow and magnificent, drapes the north sky
but I cannot see it, cannot allow it, that would be
allowing another sign. And songs, songs to follow.
What songs can sing this anyway, what humming
and what phrase will now abandon me, what woman
with a gun and her fingers to her lips draw us to another
territory further north, further cold, further on,
into the mouth of the Arctic.
I'm heading to frost, to freezing,
how perhaps returning south heads to fever,
and what I'm saving for another time is all our good,
good will, so not listening, not listening
to any dangling voice or low, lifting whistle.
All the sounds gone out, all the wind died away,
I won't look, won't look at the tail of lighted dust.

III i

In the middle of afternoons driving north
on 35, stopping for a paper and a coffee,
I read the terrifying poetry of newspapers. I
notice vowels have suddenly stopped their
routine, their alarming rooms are shut,
their burning light collapsed

the wave of takeovers, mergers and restructuring
. . . swept the world's . . . blue chips rally in New York
. . . Bundesbank looms . . . Imperial Oil increases dividends
. . . tough cutbacks build confidence

Your mouth never opens to say all this.
The breathful air of words are taken. Swept, yes.
You feel your coffee turn asphalt, you look around
and your eyes hit the dirty corners of the windy store,
stray paper, stray cups, stray oil, stray fumes of gas.
Your mouth never opens, your keys look unfamiliar.

is Microsoft a rapacious plunderer . . . or a benign
benevolent giant . . . rough road ahead

Rough road ahead they say so I leave the gas
station, leaving the paper on the counter,
not listening to the woman calling me back,
my mouth full and tasteless

III ii

Where is this. Your tongue, gone cold, gone
heavy in this winter light.
On a highway burrowing north don't waste your breath.
This winter road cannot hear it and will swallow it
whole. Don't move.
This detail then, when grass leans in certain light.
In other days, blue. This, every week no matter what grows
worse you cannot say you are on the same road, green darkens
or yellows or snows or disappears. Leave me there then,
at 2 p.m. rounding 35 to the 121 hoping
never to return here.

I should have passed, gone my way.

You come to think
the next house one kilometre away might as well
be ten, it so far from love, and shouting would produce
no blood. If I believe anything it will not matter though.
Life is porous, unimaginable in the end, only substance
burning in itself, lit by the heat of touching. It's good
how we melt back into nothing.

III iii

Look, let me be specific. I have been losing roads
and tracks and air and rivers and little thoughts
and smells and incidents and a sense of myself
and fights I used to be passionate about
and don't remember. And once I lost the mechanics, no,
the meaning of dancing, and
I have been forgetting everything, friends, and pain.
The body bleeds only water and fear when you survive
the death of your politics, but why don't I forget.
That island with an explosive at the beginning of its name
keeps tripping me and why don't I recall my life
in detail because I was always going somewhere else
and what I was living was unimportant for the while

Rough Road Ahead

let me say that all the classrooms should be burned
and all this paper abandoned like dancing and the gas
stations heading north, and all the independents
who wasted time arguing and being superior, pulling out
dictionaries and refereed journals, new marxists, neo-marxists,
independent marxists, all of us loving our smartness, oh jeez,
the arguments filling auditoriums and town halls with
smartness, taking our time with smartness for serious study,
committing suicide blowing saxophones of smartness, going
home, which windy night on Bloor Street knowing full well and
waking up shaky until smartness rings the telephone with
another invitation and postmortem about last night's meeting.
Then I lost, well, gave up the wherewithal

III iv

One gleeful headline drives me to the floor, kneeling,
and all paint turns to gazette paper and all memory
collides into photographs we could not say happened,
that is us, that's what we did. When you lose you become
ancient but this time no one will rake over these bodies
gently collecting their valuables, their pots, their hearts
and intestines, their papers and what they could bury.
This civilisation will be dug up to burn all its manifestos.
No tender archaeologist will mend our furious writings
concluding, "They wanted sweat to taste sweet, that is all,
some of them played music for nothing, some of them
wrote poems to tractors, rough hands, and rough roads,
some sang for no reason at all to judge by their condition."

III v

After everything I rely on confusion. I listen for
disaster, a storm in the Gulf of Mexico, arctic air
wreathing the whole of this unblessed continent,
mud slides burying the rich in California and the
devil turned in on himself in Oklahoma. And others,
and more than my desire reminding me that someone
used to say when I was a child don't wish for bad
you might get it, your own face might be destroyed,
you will call trouble on yourself and on your own house.
How I watch, like someone without a being, the whole
enterprise come to zero and my skin not even able
to count on itself. Still, with snow coming, counting
by the slate sky, I hope for cars and hands to freeze,
lines and light to fall, since what I've learned,
the lie of it, is no amount of will can change it. There
are whole countries exhausted for it, whole villages,
whole arms, whole mornings and whole hearts burning.
And what I wish for is natural and accidental

ALL THAT HAS HAPPENED SINCE

Arani, I meet my old friend at Arani. Arani is a piece of what
someone carried all the way here from Kerala and set down on
Spadina, all he might cull of where he came from is commerce
now, is laid out in trays hurriedly set on fire. So Arani, I sit with
my old friend at Arani, my old friend. Between us there's a boy,
his son he hasn't seen, a friendship I'm holding for ransom until
he does. Who loves a Black boy? I ask him. It's not hard to
abandon him, whole cities have. So this between us, I meet my
old friend at Arani, his whole head soaked in that teardrop off
the chin of India, or is this the way we've learned to look at it,
the teardrop, the pearl dangling on the imperial necklace. We sit
at Arani, I know about necklaces, archipelagos, and in some
lurching talk he jumps over the Indian Ocean, back and forth,
the north full of armed Tigers, tea workers, the south, treachery,
prime ministers and generals, and here the telephone calls of
more fracture and more of the same, wife beatings in St. James
Town, men I'm certain cook with too much pepper because at
home they never cooked and now only remember pepper.
I could be wrong I admit but still, and yes the boy who could do
with or without him, his head boiled in all we should have
been on those islands failing us because who ever had a chance
to say how it might be and our own particular vanity and
smallness, hatreds thinning our mouths and yellowing our
fingers. This we suspect. On any given day, he says,

there are seven hundred Asian maids in their embassies in
Kuwait, right now there are three hundred Sri Lankan maids
hiding in the Sri Lankan embassy in Kuwait, that bulwark of
American democracy, he says, a British ornithologist pursued a
rare owl for years following it to a village in the south of India,
there the ornithologist wept, distraught as villagers captured the
bird, cooked and ate it, there were lots of these birds around they
said, lots, the ornithologist wept, look, he says, I know you say
they're all in it but Chandrika is caught between the generals,
and the boy, I say, what about him adding my own disagreements,
he gets local prices in Tobago, he goes to bars at night there and
dances, they think he is a local, you know it doesn't matter this
Chandrika, the generals, her mother, Bandaranaike before,
they're all the same class, they have tea together, all you can
count on is their benevolence, how they got up this morning,
and that's no revolution, anyway we will never win now. I
hardly know why I'm fighting any more, "we," my we, taking
most of the world in my mouth, we, between my lips, the
mouth of the world is open, the boy's mother told me her
mother called menstruation. The mouth of the world is open
she'd say. Anyway I was driving here and you can't believe this
city, man, it is filthy and look at you, year in year out hoping
about someplace else, you ever wonder why don't we live here
ay, why don't we live here, by the way the Sri Lankans cannot
hope to beat the West Indies at cricket, don't make yourself
think about it you'll only be disappointed;

they're all the same, why are you hoping, I say, all the same class
and the Americans have them, you think anything will pass
now, peaceful solution, negotiating, look someone whispered
something to the Tigers and they got up from the table, a mistake,
a mistake, he wags, man, they want them dead, this class has only
disdain, man, you should read Balzac, he skips, Balzac was
saying these things, it's incredible, riffing conspiratorially at
Arani as if he's talking about arms caches, Balzac is incredible,
there is going to be another massive offensive, they're going to
kill everyone. The pope wants to beatify Queen Isabella, I tell
him, and has made thirty-three saints and seven hundred
blesseds, do you realise just how absurd we are here sitting at
Arani, and the boy, JFK's rocking chair sold for 450,000 dollars
and European neo-fascists are glamour boys in the *New York
Times*, do we realise they are more afraid of communists
than fascists, that is not good news for us. I sit here and listen
to radios, I hear their plots, and stagger, and the boy, well all
there is is the boy, just like any ordinary person, we are not
revolutionaries, we were never drawn into wars, we never
slept on our dirty fingers and pissed in our clothes, why, why
didn't we do that, but here, here we grind our teeth on our stone
hearts and foretell and mistake, and jump around the world in
our brains. Whether we are right is unimportant now, Leningrad
is St. Petersburg and God is back in vogue, this is the future. I've
forgotten how to dance with him, something heavy is all in my
mouth, I get exhausted at Arani, my eyes reach for something
domestic, the mop in the Kerala man's hand, well, the boy is still
between us, and all the wars we've pried open and run our
tongues over like dangerous tin cans.

IV ii

in the middle of traffic at Church and Gerrard I notice someone,
two women, for a moment unfamiliar, not crouched with me
in a hallway, for this moment unfamiliar, not cringing at the
grit of bombers, the whine of our breath in collapsing chests, in
the middle of traffic right there for a moment unfamiliar and
familiar, the light changing and as usual in the middle of almost
dying, yelling phone numbers and parting, feeling now, as the
light beckons, all the delicateness of pedestrians. I wish that I
was forgetful. All that day the streets felt painful and the
subways tender as eggshells.

IV iii

a Sunday, soft as any, plays with its eyelash,
brushing its cheek over Petit Trou, Rushdie's
archangel, Lennox and Seddon's "The trees
and flowers of the Caribbean" – *lignum vitae,*
cassia fistula, passiflora, alpina purpurata –
lay on the table, soft and falling as any,
a man with a cutlass severs the doorway
in two, language, politics, frangipani grab
the lungs, sweeter than air, a familiar foot
in brown like a friend and yellow like the fading
light, soft Sunday, just as she puts away
the camera and returns to Gibreel, the
movie star and jacaranda, how it flowers,
his hand, its lines ruffled, brushes her mouth
and she hears baying louder than the ocean,
hoarse as any desert and Vargas Llosa's prophet.

by now it's just between evening and night
and just to his left a copybook page of a sky,
water and pen ink blotting, the neighbour
is watering her plants, ixora and fern, bringing
in the mats from sunning, thinking, just a
woman baying, his arm gauzed, she thinks,
in dried banana bark, ending in the cutlass,
his face gauzed, his hand brushes her mouth,
baying, all the particles of fear and dust and
throat phlegm, and the evening coming,
baying, she hears the fierce branches of her
lungs bay thick as storms, soft as any Sunday
here, she already feels the slice of her head,
dead as stones, hoarse as seeds.

all is wonder at this moment, what calculation
does he make, she wonders, waiting for the light
to brood, willing the doorway he will cut in two,
willing it to stay open, the woman alone inside
sated on Sunday's soft temple thinking the world
is perfect, what account has he settled, has he weighed
her heart, weighed his own, then decided, yes, the cutlass,
oxidised on coconut coir, wild meat and gloricida tangle,
the obeah she'll see in banana gauze, his bare hand,
for her mouth, yes, the shallows at Petit Trou
where he'll wash the cutlass if it comes to that, watch
the salt froth her blood and the tide take it, where
he'll say some prayers anyway for himself and cross
his chest with the same hand. Did he calculate
anything, that she might reach up to his hand, baying

adding groan, slate wings and the sand her neck
already feels drizzling on Petit Trou, she decides,
she is dead already, already dead, chopped, so he sees
a dead woman baying, soft, soft, yes, the Sunday
growing older, the brittle ear, the pebbled throat,
the bone lungs, her mouth wide like the sea, and she
moving his hand, thinking, out, out the door he is
cutting in two and already dead, she wills herself
out to the verandah, he is in her way, that is all,
and she moves on baying now not on her legs,
the sea at Petit Trou is outside lapping, on a day
when there are no clouds she can see another island
clear, clear through soft Atlantic mist and he is in her
way and killed her already, her head cracked in splinters

she is closer now so the cutlass will drop or not,
but she heads into the red lump of her death, now
he cannot stop her baying, she reaches the sea
and he runs but she is still bellowing, cannot stop
and he all gauze, all calculation, all cutlass, runs
runs soft, soft and disappears,
the taste of rice is with her followed by the taste
of metal, corks followed by the taste of rust, the
taste of nails, the taste of buttercups, the taste
of rings, the taste of bark, the baying brays in the
car the next morning, riding Patience Hill,
walking the sea spray at Petit Trou, walking
as if she is walking the first time, the taste of crisp
bees, the stings in the fat of her cheek, the taste
of aloes, the lifting sea steam, the day, parched
at her eyes, parched open, what did he count
on, his finger peeling skin, waiting for the day to sit
closer to the door he would cut and break every
other day she had in two, cut Sunday brief as stones.

what did he count on, the things she can't collect
and put back right, the bees, the scissors and radio
and rice and nails now everywhere but in their
proper place, the box for this and that and beaks
and rings and wire netting upside down, her new
need for smooth clean surfaces, the revulsion she
notices for dust, the chairs she wants to hold on
her head to save them from imagined water, the
afternoon she drives Black Rock, Ibo Gully, Les
Coteaux to see if they're still there and they're not,
except like gravel breaking in her mouth.

IV iv

I saw three Sikh men early the next morning, the avenue wind
swept and pelting ice, the morning dark even if light had made
it so, going from mailbox to mailbox delivering news about
meat sales, vegetable bargains. They were silent, waving to each
other, why three of them one old, one in the middle of his life,
one boy duty all over him, and why I think their lives would not
be just so somewhere else but bless them in other thoughts just
for here.

the girl starts the morning too, ragged like years
ahead of her, she is a translator of languages
and souls, she waits for the bus, her Walkman
in a war with the pages she's been handed,
her mother's face, her brother's face, the bus
driver's face, and the sign for starvation, the sign
for music, the one for reprisals, she'll read and ignore
them and turn her Walkman loud enough to curdle
the liquid in her eardrums that turns every music
to its rightful metronome of iron foot rings, bracelets.
This. You will read nothing in her own face now. She
is a translator of bureaucracies. This race passes through
her, ledgers and columns of thirst, notebooks of bitter
feeling, this street she's arrived at waiting for the bus
is only one. All night she's been up dancing in her room,
keeping out her mother, barring the doorway with bass,
she's feeding on genius, so till, the girl starts the morning,
weary on the floor, wisdom is what's keeping her up, she's
a noticiary of pain, that faculty is overgrown in her until
it is all she conducts, she's an electrician, pure electricity
flows through her, her fingertips are disappearing in sheer
lightning.

IV vi

a Baptist priestess preaches to a sidewalk in this city
and if this city could take it she would look into its eyes
but everyone, me too, glides by,
all who might pronounce her sane run ahead,
drive quickly before she catches our eyes,
and she is mad, thinking god could find her here,
and in her eyes that is her penance I suppose,
to talk to the pavement at Oakwood and St. Clair
and ours to avoid her as if we suddenly lost
consciousness of race and what she's calling for,
all eyes instead drop to the sash of dirt around her waist
and say "for god's sake, these people could embarrass you, ay!"
her husband left her, took all her money
after she worked to bring him here, well after all
who else could explain but the pavement dense with answers

IV vii

11 p.m. to 7 a.m. she worked years leaving them in this apartment
and that, and how she could, bringing them one at a time,
picking them up by airplane where she had left them
in this village, that town, this family, which aunt and grandmother
and never being able to reach them as she had left them,
how folded in brown paper was not how you left children,
untying sweet string was not how they came, and whatever
plans she had others had plenty more, and the doorway would
finally burst open and the walls let in the road and every thanks
ended up a curse and her own habits come to haunt her,
this girl once sewing a yard of children to a V-necked dress,
then it was over, all speech that granted her a steady shape
as what a woman was supposed to be, all dress and hips,
all spirit and animality, that left, then everything for them,
and the stitching going badly, on her hands she noticed
numbness to hot water and hot pans, a lamentation in her back
from lifting spoiled white bodies, their own whimpering death
songs elegising, "bitch, black bitch, I want my own daughter."

IV viii

in Chechnya, a Russian plane has dropped a bomb on a village
the radio says, I just heard, ten billion to Yeltsin
from the IMF, just today, just like any South American darling
devoted sonofabitch, I know this is no news, nor walls
of photographs of children in Bukavu, tents of refugees
in Goma, it's their own fault, before it was communism
now they just don't know how to work the gift of capitalism,
all of us want to fly to America right now, right away please
and Americans wonder why, feel we must love them
that's why, we're just jealous, that's why, we just want
to steal what they have, thief from thief make god laugh,
so I'm getting into the business of false passports and new
identities, I'm taking in conferences on pomo-multiplicity,
the everyday world, the signifying monkey, the post-colonial
moment, the Michigan militia, cyberspace, come to think of it
give each fleeing Hutu/Tutsi a home page, subalterns of their
own, I'm going to Bukavu with Windows

IV ix

what exactly is the difference between these groups, perplexed
the host, well nothing ideological, says the expert, well why in
the new world aren't they getting along, communism's gone,
no proxy wars, no real role for cia agents, soviet spies,
what in the world is going on down there then,
well it's hard to say really, the krahn, the croats, the serbs,
the shia, the hutu, you see, the falasha, the hezbollah, well
democracy's run amuck, but what is it, the host wants to know
and the expert can no longer reach for anything
but family disagreements and old forbidden grudges let loose
by all that voting and free speech, the old underdeveloped
don't have the same level of sophistication as us
and what about Russia, Poland, don't tell me they would vote
back the commies, not yet used to democracy, the market forces,
they don't understand, the thing is we've resurrected some
demons

IV x

here is the history of the body;
water perhaps darkness perhaps stars
bone then scales then wings then legs then arms
then belly then bone then nerves then feathers then scales,
then wings then liquid then pores then bone
then blood pouring, then eyes, then distance, only this,
all that has happened since is too painful,
too unimaginable

"I never saw Managua when miniskirts were in," Ortega
wrote in prison and newsprint bleeds with weeping
the walls of this room weep, a Saturday weeps,
what do we make of it, a miniskirt measuring
time, senses missed, dates, a life and people walking
in streets and thoughts as you walk along that are taken
for granted and forgotten at the end of a journey,
Ortega sitting in his cell could not have these
but had we given another shape to bodies
as well as theory and poems and speeches
what would we have missed and wept for and forgotten

Remembering Miranda's campaigns as if he were there
and Bolivar as if fighting for his own life and Jose Marti
like a son grown from a pebble tossed in the Caribbean basin
a comrade in his last speech and his last hope
ignites the hall in Montreal,
he is the one left alive and left here
he is a stranger in another millennium, in another room
with his passion and his shimmering ancestry,
a question from the back of the hall about armed struggle,
he has been waiting,
he sticks his grapple in its rock face and there's
a ruthlessness in him, a touch of the old sexy revolutionary,
and he stumbles on now, then his hand touches a greying chin
and it is as if he is startled and ashamed
and unable to land in now, all left undone.
There is a sign that he must make us,
the shape of the one thing that he has never written, ever

we stumble on the romance of origins,
some stories we all love like sleep, poured in our mouths like
milk. How far we've travelled now, still we stoop at a welcome
fire and hum, to a stick stringed with hair, our miscalculations,
we return to the misology in heat and loneliness, the smell of
meat and hunger

here again the history of the body
men romance the shape they're in
the mythologies they attach to it
their misunderstandings
and this is what James should have said to Trotsky
as they drank in Mexico City,
what might have happened if one had said to the other,
comrade, this is the time you betray the body

nearly late, we are in a hall waiting for a gesture,
Ortega out of prison if his prison is not the whole
of South America now, Jose Marti's son if the hall in Montreal
is not his coffin,
we are waiting for some language to walk into
like a large house
with no rooms and no quarter
all waiting for his signal
we happen on what was wrong in the first place,
how the intangible took over,
the things left in a language with carelessness or purpose,
men's arms and legs and belly, their discreet assignments
and regulations
the things kept secret with a hand pressed to the mouth
by priests, judges, mullahs
this way they resist what they must become
full knowing that we must throw our life away
and all impressions of ourselves.
Comrades, perhaps this is what you might whisper
on the telephone to the young men who adore you still,
"Goodbye, then. And well . . . betray your body."

IV xi

That damn corridor, green with half dead guerrillas
and want to be guerrilla just shut in and might as well
did blow up with we in it, the life it throw we into
is the same scrambling as before and only the magic once
or twice is remembering how it change we.
When we meet now we say, "It was the best years
of my life. I wouldn't exchange it for youth." Hustling European
guests into a hotel, pain stroking a face with the wrong answer
for the cause of the end of we. Watching only through a plane
window at Point Salines and busy not recalling where we was
rightly, eating coconut ice cream at the bar in Crown Point,
starting all over with hardly any heart. For different reason
all of we, everyone the bridge over. Over the exhaust
of them hilly hilly street and the blazing sun like fire,
fire in we tail, it wasn't enough that we had was to find a way
to love for once, we love it hard enough and hard
was how everything was as if it design, once bad mind America,
and bad mind had to come, why that, as if we know it long, long
as though we expect, well it easy after all to notice the worse, any
body would fail to see how it could fix, mortar break, pestle break

I sit down in the bar myself, in a lot of bar, if I could drink
my way dead I would but my stomach give out before my heart

IV xii

why this voice rank and ready to be called bitter again, liquor
doesn't soothe it and books either, self saboteur, it could be nice
and grateful but Fanon had it, native envy, watery and long as
that bloody sea, envy for everything then, kitchen knives their
dullness or sharpness, shoes their certainty, envelopes their
letters, clocks their lag, paper its clarity, envy to the participle and
adverb, the way they own being, ripe envy full as days, and
breasts, bony as wardrobes, old as babies

IV xiii

for only one moment it spreads on the table like water
and heat, its light piercing the heavy, heavy weight of this sky,
it moves my now inanimate body, all stone, moves it
to sound and leaves; how small things stir me, sunlight
between two high-rise buildings, the looked and looked for
possibility of a leaf on a dormant tree, how I forget
whatever thoughts I have that follow a logic, whatever
impulse in me that wanted satisfaction, now days, their whims
and changeableness have me in a grip, the sky is a pain.
I was always for succumbing to something bigger,
I wanted something unindividual like distance or chaff,
or the spinning silence in the air after blue-grey tanagers,
signal and undifferent as obsidian caves bluing and blacking,
tracks of country uncompeting, and braids, hair latched
handful over handful. I had hoped that some billowy humid
night swooning to its knees, the smell of coconut smoke
or some cold night cracking silence into its middle
with the smell of wood smoke . . . it would occur to me,
that nothing was wrong.

LAND TO LIGHT ON

V i

Maybe this wide country just stretches your life to a thinness
just trying to take it in, trying to calculate in it what you must
do, the airy bay at its head scatters your thoughts like someone
going mad from science and birds pulling your hair, ice invades
your nostrils in chunks, land fills your throat, you are so busy
with collecting the north, scrambling to the Arctic so wilfully, so
busy getting a handle to steady you to this place you get blown
into bays and lakes and fissures you have yet to see, except
on a map in a schoolroom long ago but you have a sense that
whole parts of you are floating in heavy lake water heading for
what you suspect is some other life that lives there, and you, you
only trust moving water and water that reveals itself in colour. It
always takes long to come to what you have to say, you have to
sweep this stretch of land up around your feet and point to the
signs, pleat whole histories with pins in your mouth and guess
at the fall of words.

V ii

But the sight of land has always baffled you,
there is dirt somewhere older than any exile
and try as you might, your eyes only compose
the muddy drain in front of the humid almond
tree, the unsettling concrete sprawl of the housing
scheme, the stone your uncle used to smash his name
into another uncle's face, your planet is your hands,
your house behind your eyebrows and the tracing
paper over the bead of islands of indifferent and
reversible shapes, now Guadeloupe is a crab pinched
at the waist, now Nevis' borders change by mistake
and the carelessness of history, now sitting in Standard
Five, the paper shifting papery in the sweat of your
fingers you come to be convinced that these lines will
not matter, your land is a forced march on the bottom
of the Sargasso, your way tangled in life

V iii

I am giving up on land to light on, it's only true, it is only
something someone tells you, someone you should not trust
anyway. Days away, years before, a beer at your lips and the view
from Castara, the ocean as always pulling you towards its bone
and much later, in between, learning to drive the long drive
to Burnt River, where the land is not beautiful, braised
like the back of an animal, burnt in coolness, but the sky is,
like the ocean pulling you toward its bone, skin falling away
from your eyes, you see it without its history of harm, without
its damage, or everywhere you walk on the earth there's harm,
everywhere resounds. This is the only way you will know
the names of cities, not charmed or overwhelmed, all you see is
museums of harm and metros full, in Paris, walls inspected
crudely for dates, and Amsterdam, street corners full of
druggists, ashen with it, all the way from Suriname, Curaçao,
Dutch and German inking their lips, pen nibs of harm blued in
the mouth, not to say London's squares, blackened in statues,
Zeebrugge, searching the belly of fish, Kinshasa, through an
airplane window the dictator cutting up bodies grips the plane
to the tarmac and I can't get out to kiss the ground

V iv

This those slaves must have known who were my mothers, skin
falling from their eyes, they moving toward their own bone,
"so thank god for the ocean and the sky all implicated, all
unconcerned," they must have said, "or there'd be nothing to
love." How they spent a whole lifetime undoing the knot
of a word and as fast it would twirl up again, spent
whole minutes inching their eyes above sea level only
for latitude to shift, only for a horrible horizon to list, thank god
for the degrees of the chin, the fooling plane of a doorway, only
the mind, the not just simple business of return and turning,
that is for scholars and indecisive frigates, circling and circling,
stripped in their life, naked as seaweed, they would have sat
and sunk but no, the sky was a doorway, a famine and a jacket,
the sea a definite post

V v

I'm giving up on land to light on, slowly, it isn't land,
it is the same as fog and mist and figures and lines
and erasable thoughts, it is buildings and governments
and toilets and front door mats and typewriter shops,
cards with your name and clothing that comes undone,
skin that doesn't fasten and spills and shoes. It's paper,
paper, maps. Maps that get wet and rinse out, in my hand
anyway. I'm giving up what was always shifting, mutable
cities' fluorescences, limbs, chalk curdled blackboards
and carbon copies, wretching water, cunning walls. Books
to set it right. Look. What I know is this. I'm giving up.
No offence. I was never committed. Not ever, to offices
or islands, continents, graphs, whole cloth, these sequences
or even footsteps

V vi

Light passes through me lightless, sound soundless,
smoking nowhere, groaning with sudden birds. Paper
dies, flesh melts, leaving stockings and their useless vanity
in graves, bodies lie still across foolish borders.
I'm going my way, going my way gleaning shade, burnt
meridians, dropping carets, flung latitudes, inattention,
screeching looks. I'm trying to put my tongue on dawns
now, I'm busy licking dusk away, tracking deep twittering
silences. You come to this, here's the marrow of it, not
moving, not standing, it's too much to hold up, what I
really want to say is, I don't want no fucking country, here
or there and all the way back, I don't like it, none of it,
easy as that. I'm giving up on land to light on, and why not,
I can't perfect my own shadow, my violent sorrow, my
individual wrists.

DIALECTICS

VI i

I feel like my aunt hunkered to a foot that wouldn't
cure, her hair tightened to a "dougla" wave and her mouth
sweet on laughter and paradise plums, she could fry fish
and make it taste sweet, sweet after her seasoning
rubbed the silvery red skin on snapper and she could turn
flour into sweet bread glazed with crystalled sugar water,
bread carved in steamy yeast and butter, her hands parted
a corn row clean clean and ribbons bounced white and blue
satin to her fingers, she liked to sweeten up, perfume
cheap as pennies richened on her skin and her one good leg
slender and tapered to the ankle she braceleted against
the whispers of bad woman, she dressed in tight skirts and low
backer bodices, taught us the jive spinning and dipping
between the Morris chairs to Count Basie but she could not
knead that leaky leg well. I woke up to her sitting in the dark,
the corners of the living room warm and amber with floor
polish, moaning and rubbing her foot. She didn't sleep,
she sat up, her leg on a chair waiting for daylight
to turn corn meal into porridge with cinnamon spice and
vanilla essence, or roll it into fig leaves with raisins, to repeat
the lesson of the jive when we got home at three and to quarrel
about our hair, flying away free which she'd pulled back smart
in rubber bands just this morning.

VI ii

I had thought my life wider, had counted on my cleverness
at noticing not just her sweet hand but her sore leg and
congratulated myself even then on analysing the dialectic,
the turned corn meal, the amber pain hanging at my Aunt
Phyllis' foot. I liked detail. The way she dismissed her leg in
daring dresses, the way she hung and fingered the fine gold
chain around her good ankle, the idea that she refused to give
up any of her senses as tragic as they were, she wanted a sweet
life to balance out, to complete her fiery anklet, even at seventy
with a heart attack under anaesthesia she says, girl, I tired of this
foot all the time all the time so, she risks another skin graft and
she wore gold rings and loved guipure lace and sweet men
named Casimir on motorcycles, she loved the way they glittered
past savannah grass, how envy soaked other women's Sundays,
for him, but she with her aching foot sat astride his back,
the cut of her dresses deep to the ripple of her waist.
At fifty she married a man who was possessive and selfish
and she loved that too.

VII i

I took in the child sucking her thumb, holding on to the butter
of her mother's skirt, the other sitting on the gathers at his
mother's hips, leaning out dangerously, leaning away happily
from the mother's set cheek, set mouth and the baby in the
remaining arm, matter in her eyes, screaming. I made a note.
One at her dress tail, one on her hip, one in her arm. I made a
note of the guard answering reluctantly, and the barricade to
the electricity company, he so used to answering indifferently to
women on Fridays, "He gone, he not here, don't waste your
time," the yellow trucks laden with men barely missing her feet,
and her neck whipping swift, piercing the benches of them for
his face. I never fell into the heaviness of babies. Thank god. Not
me and no baby. Baby, in my bony lap? It can't hold no baby
there. I is not nobody mother. I made a note of what she choked
back, her spit dry, her face hardening and hardening and
hmmning, chewing reedy on their laughter, their laughter here
cracking the dust of their faces and boots, their laughter here
rattling in the can of the truck like uneven stone, heating it like
cigarette butts, like men coughing catarrh at some joke that
burns their chests too.

VII ii

Their laughter here where laughter is to
sew up harm or just like harm where somehow
there is blame in it, mockery for landing there
at the guard's impatience, the barricade's iron denial,
a man's whim and no mercy, it so despise itself, I did
not miss her skin setting over its shame, her jaw
making another plan, her shifting the child from
hip to ground, from ground to hip unable to make
anything of the baby's indecision to yawn or bawl, I
could not miss the marl of her teeth crushed on worry,
nothing she could sell for nothing, at the end of herself,
needing a plan because at the end of herself she was
still alive, still blooming children and crying, and short
of burying them in the cane field at the back of her house
she had to hang them on her hips where harm
was greater if only they knew the sweet ground would
be milk.

VII iii

I saw her head up the road toward
the evening coming, that road, the same
as when its name was Carib, cut
in the San Fernando hill, that evening
as unconcerned as any for her, bent
on its own gluttony, she, like an ancient
woman with her regular burdens heading
into a hill. I saw her begin again,
the coming dark slipping between her legs
and disappearing into which century past.
I saw her shoulder the dark like another child
and consider its face, its waiting mouth
closed on her breast.
She told me once she loved babies, hated
to see them grow up, she missed
their babyness, that's why she had so many.
I saw her heading up a road into a hill
with her vanity and her lust
not for any man in an electric company truck
but for her own face.

VII iv

I took no time in the rose light of
the sun departing the hill, her dress turning
ochre and melting, the child at her skirt
looking back and looking alone after the mist
of the mother disappearing into the going
light. This peace filled in evening smoke
of evening pots cooking so much or so little
on this Carib road, and her mouth springing
water and drying at the thought of her own shack
at the head of a cane field smokeless.
This peace swallowing a woman, three children
and a road, this peace closing ochre on vermilion
on utter, utter darkness where sleep is enough food
at least and she could fool those children
to a sleep cooing a watery promise of nice things
tomorrow, ladling sugar water into their mouths
and then sleepless waiting for his sodden body to fall
and lay near the steps outside or break a window
coming in.

VII v

Her burning head, not just how they
would eat but how she would love, why
was it only lost to her this need to love, how
it was jumbled up and when the children
were asleep the handle of it slipped her,
and with rum in her head she felt it crack
her bones, howl her voice to a scream.
She pedalled the Hitachi sewing machine
for kilometres into the cane field
over the night fields soughing soft past
other roads through long savannahs
and houses choked on sleep, wet tablelands
and thick dirt smells, rushed to wet sand
clenching the sea at Plaisance, Mayaro,
her feet delirious. In the morning
the bedclothes would be a dress and a skirt
and a jacket and a blouse, kilometres
of pedalling and it was hard to breathe night,
holding it in her fierce lungs, her feet
losing bone, she hummed the needle through
the presser foot singing like rain.

VIII i

once they take we to a dance, the both of
them, the three of we, nine, ten, twelve,
pull we to the dance floor thundering
with big people dancing to steelband
and perfume and something serious in
their dancing, something that didn't want
no interruption from two foolish aunts
and some children they bring to a dance
but they was laughing and pulling
we on the dance floor saying,
"All yuh want to come to dance, well dance."
They bundle we on a bench in a corner
to sleep when sleep overcome we fastness
and they danced, wining and shimmying
to Lord Kitchener.
I didn't know no dance could be so dark
and full of serious desire that frighten me
no arse. A lady and a man not even holding
tight but some tightness holding them, her
white low-heeled shoes on the inside of his
black ones and her shoulders shine shine fire
in the shadow of more people, she look lush
at the same time as well . . . serious is all I
could say, a school teacher serious but let go,
wasn't no school teacher red red so glowing
on the dance floor

and they laugh at we, lifting we up and taking
we home, "Is dance all yuh want to dance."

VIII ii

that night we wanted to fly in our aunts' skin,
we so loved their talk, the sugar in their mouths,
they were always laughing, throwing water over
their shoulders and going on anyway, the one
with five children stealing out the door without them
after she'd fed them and oiled them or perhaps not,
but slipping out the door going looking for another
as her mother said; trusting the cane field, at the bottom
of Cocoyea village asleep behind the house, at her back,
blue in the black black night, to put those children
to sleep too and keep them while she found another,
tall and pretty, who would bend into the well of her cheeks,
clutch the bone of them like a carnivore, five children
and she could still laugh the best men into the dough
of her skirt and love them so hard a ship to England
would leave without her many times and leave the wharf
without the suitcase full of dresses sewn for months
piled on the Hitachi machine, mouthsful of needles
and thread bristling and black cake packed for sisters
abroad, waiting for news and hungry for such skirts,
such love themselves, her mother and father waiting
in disappointment and dread until there was no way
she would make that ship.

VIII iii

She came later, weeks, months, said she was sick,
suddenly struck just so by illness, god, just so,
a headache, a pain, an arm that just wouldn't move
just that morning when she woke up, a stroke,
missed the boat by minutes, imagine, just, minutes,
or laughing with no explanation, or just something
told her not to go, bad spirits, obeah, the child' father
other woman, must be, any promise no matter how
meagre but was a sign anyway. She came minutes
after the ship set sail anyhow, feigning simple lateness
and horror and vowing to pay back every cent they'd saved
and lost on the ship cutting the water, glittering like hard
diamonds, sloughing the jetty. She could not resist,
in all her crocodile tears and some real too, a deep voice
calling her away from her mother and her father, calling
her away from their disappointment, across the wharf,
a hollow dark cheek calling her, "Wha' happenin', girl,
you scarce like gold." She could not help laughing and turning
away from the bedraggled mother and father to answer
the cunning hint in gold, of her loveliness, "Oh gord, dahlin'
wha' happenin'? Where the fete, where the fete?"

VIII iv

She came in a hurry to leave, "Keep the children
for me, mama. I hear about a work." Bustling
sweetly dressed like she was going to a party, kissing
the children promising them sweeties if they behaved
for mama. She wore pink powder and dabbed
the puff on our faces, exquisite dust clouds
of perfume exploding, we squealed with love
and terror. Where she went, we wanted to go.
It was some place you had to hurry to and something
hot and sweet was going on there and waiting for you,
knowledge. What was it that she had to keep going to
and was more seductive than a ship going away
and returning into another life, not a bucket
under the leak of a bachie, the man with promises gone,
not fright at a failed abortion, the blood endless
in a small room, what was so sweet in all that running
racket, in men grinding the hills of her cheeks to gravel,
panning her eyes for their brittle rages.

that night we wanted to fly into our aunts' skins,
the one, look her voice I cannot tell you but you
would have to know the meaning of shade
and water to understand it, you would have to
know night to recognise it rippling and coconut oil,
she had a voice meant to describe darkness
and daylight, only slippery and burning like Vat 19
rum, it could sound like a ribbon yards and yards
long and red over the counter of Lloyd's shop
round the corner, a ribbon glistening
over the barrels of pig's tails and salt fish,
such a voice like food and air. She rescued me across
the road from that shop, bawling at Miss Greenidge's
private school. "Is child you want to beat?" she honeyed
high and dangerous, "Why you don't go and make
child, eh?" grabbing the guava stick from Miss Greenidge.
One time Reds and them who was bad-johns, their whole
family, mother and everything, Reds ride a bicycle right
at me and I fall in the canal full of nasty water where
you could catch wabeen and everybody garbage, well
my aunt just get a piece a wood and gone up to Reds'
house just so. Reds en't even come out, mother and
everything. I had uncle too but them aunts was like tree
and good cloth, river and big road. She, with the voice
would bring me fried snapper all the way from the country
by the sea because I was sad. Who could tell sadness
in a child. Who could tell it wasn't just this morning's
slight or flying need, who could tell it wasn't just the
hunger of children for everything. I've never done that
for anyone, just so, tell what was needed was snapper,
fried crisp and silver red and answering whatever loneliness.
Her smile was wet and warming and one little finger
had a gold ring on it and both hands were small and nothing
was unhappy in them

IX i

god I watched you all, watched and watched and in the end
could not say a word to you that was not awkward and insulting,
there was really no way to describe you and what I wanted
to say came out stiff and old as if I could not trust you
to understand my new language which after all I had made
against you, against the shapes of your bodies, against your
directions, your tongues, the places your feet took you, how I
know holding in everything, warm breath and silence and
words because of you and waiting, how you watched me watch
and did not say all that my eyes said was distance and blame
and something superior, yet you offered me food for Christmas
and laughter and your life, your news across the telephone,
bad news, self-mockery, disappointments and things you feared,
your pilgrimages, a holy shrine at Marmora, faith, even in
its incapable saints, but you prayed, knelt in mud there anyway,
subway riders you braved, benedictions serrating your dress,
how they could not understand your belief sprouting on trains,
your sojourns in hospitals, giving over your bodies to people
who didn't care, and I was no comfort just an ear welling with
water, their mouths drowning in it, how you must have
regretted these confidences knowing I could do nothing with
them but bathe you in more blame, more sorrow. How I told you
nothing in return, pretended that my life was fine, and it was,
thinking, no policemen were at my door, no sons drowning in
their own brains, none of my daughters without a way out
how I told you nothing in return, my life was fine

and nothing touched me and it didn't, how I was so far away from you by then and these conversations scared me. I am not good at anything except standing still like a wall, my only instinct is do nothing, avoid notice, and even when I believe so soundly in dialectics I look over my shoulder for wicked spirits, making my whole being logged in its inert self, how it was not you, not you but something holding us all, more than this understanding we are caught in can say, how the circumference of this world grips us to this place, how its science works, how it will take a change of oceans shaking the other way

If I could think of what I'd meant again, and seas; I never
developed any signs except sleep, nothing to know me by,
I kept to myself brewing ways to sit and close the door
and not touch anything that may fall and left you to living
because what is the point of seeing so much it stills you, as, yes,
oceans, how we give each other up for whatever concentration
we lack, the complete ruin a thought would present, how
explosive the untangling of eyelashes can be if say they open
on this, how so much depends on sleep, worlds and streets
and briefcases and half hours, and gardens and glass windows
and shoe leather and white shirts and sugar all balanced on
our sleeping, so much depends on sleep, so much induces it, all
the danger it prevents, iron pots tumbling and seams of blood
opening under cutlasses, what I'd meant again was so much
depends on a woman sitting with her hands in her lap, so
much on deciding to wait in the road for a motorcycle, a bus,
so much disappears on a road, cries and sets off again. I know
it is from small things that we know anything, why it did not
strike me to live as they did, how I watched instead and knew
something bad was waiting there, right there in the middle
of their laughing, right there when they hurried to the next
desire, how my breath would stop at something careening
in them. No I didn't want their life and I wanted their life
because they didn't know that they were living it and I envied
them that. I envied them that and I burned to wake up bright
not noticing days where I noticed them most and where
their news would sink into the front door and the walls fall off
the house, the way a skirt is no protection, days crawling until
my life is there whatever I think.

X

In the church yard which was the cemetery, the savannah
whining grass and heat, the weekdays loud with work, and
Sunday quiet raged like fever. Here I felt discomfort draw
in my body like blood and me drawn out of them. I wanted to fly
into their skins and I wanted to escape them. Sundays were a
weight against my chest, the weight of pebbles against birds
and green fruit and small ponds. Sundays crept. And in their
slowness, in all the time they gave, opening their dry palms
giving as if they could ever be generous, in all that time, not
noticing that they were passing sentence on us and giving us
breath to watch and burn slowly, in all the time they drew,
in the slowness of churches, the slowness of black serge, the slow
papery scent from the bible, the slowness of stockings, the slow
hiss of hot combs braising hair, in the slow, slow slowness
which is not ease, in the starch slowness of crinoline, in the waiting
slowness of soft asphalt roads, the looking long gazing slowness
of the curve and depth of more and more road, slow purple
quietness of cocoa pods, the high cracking slowness of parrots,
their pairness and blue blue height, the drop of the eyes
after their flight, long, long searching
unable to make anything of how they leave the earth tilting

the slowness of sand, ponderous, ponderous slowness of cricket
pitches, their struggling green and empty royal stands, the long
echo of wells, buckets, standpipes running water, lamps dried
out of kerosene and the wait at the storekeeper's beck for trust,
palms, their backs crumbling to hot ashes, wiped over mouths,
hands propping sorrow at windows, doorways, in the slow
yellow, black, red powder of butterflies, slow suffocation of
childhood, the resolute slowness of birthdays, the violent
slowness of flour, the regular ruin of storms, seas, winds,
Sundays in all their sweet time, the sugary slowness of parlours
and sweet jars, gold spit cornered slowness of mouths, in the
hoarse bray of donkeys slow, slow, skidding to slow everlastingly
slow Sunday, moths coming in to burn with gravity in the yawn
of lamp wicks, the crowded bed where we slept crosswise and
damp with someone's pee, the mattress ticking teased and
teased in the slowness of weeks and dried in the wait between
rains, the drawl of knees, elbows gashing, fighting in slow sleep
for room, in the window above our heads pulling in the cold,
wet slow rainy season, the wait and wait for January. Sundays
stretched in all their time from one to the other until I had a life
of them in their cicada whining, razor grassed stiff stiff slowing,
I knew my life come still like a heart waiting at the reed of itself.

XI

no I do not long, long, slowly for the past.
I am happy it is gone. If I long for it,
it is for the hope of it curled like burnt
paper. All the things I should have lived
slowly and content but lived grudgingly
instead, all the things still detectable in
the thin frail black of it not yet turned to
powder. All the things I should not have
noticed or breathed in, the harm, the envy,
the wreck an ocean can be in, the helpless
transparency of a street, an island, the raged
flood of a body in wood. If I long for it,
I long for it arrested, arrested among zinnias'
dust, their skins wilting in too much rain
water, their heads heavy, one moment my
feet splayed in mud and ants, stooping,
listening at returns or goings, at hours,
one moment the light finishing soft, turning
toward home thinking "ma calling," my sister
skidding down the guava tree, we laughing,
blue airmail letters opening, whisping, "Dear
mama, hope you are well and enjoying the
best of health." The corners of a house strafed
with sunlight that turns fawn and liquid, stooped
there picking up a brush or an iron. Nothing
lived longer, only this moment without disaster
in half movement on its way to movement,
half light still dark, black that is billowy
and vanishes in a hand. If I long for anything
it is shadow I long for, regions of darkness.

XII

Out of them. To where? As if I wasn't them.
To this I suppose. The choices fallen into
and unmade. Out of them. Out of shape
and glimmer and into hissing prose. What
could it mean, all that ocean, all that bush,
all that room, all that hemmed and sweet light.
Don't be mistaken, the whole exercise was
for escaping, the body cut so, the tongue cut
so, the drape of the head and the complications
boiling to their acid verbs. This pine was waiting,
this road already travelled, this sea in the back
of my head roiling its particular wrecks
and like escaping one doesn't look too close
at landing, any desert is lush, sand blooms,
any grit in the mouth is peace, the mechanics
of a hummingbird less blazing than the whirr,
all at once calligraphy and spun prism, this new
landfall when snows come and go and come again,
this landfall happened at your exact flooding and
even though you had a mind, well, landing . . .
it doesn't count on flesh or memory, or any purposes

ISLANDS VANISH

XIII

In this country where islands vanish, bodies submerge,
the heart of darkness is these white roads, snow
at our throats, and at the windshield a thick white cop
in a blue steel windbreaker peering into our car, suspiciously,
even in the blow and freeze of a snowstorm, or perhaps
not suspicion but as a man looking at aliens.
Three Blacks in a car on a road blowing eighty miles an hour
in the wind between a gas station and Chatham. We stumble
on our antiquity. The snow-blue laser of a cop's eyes fixes us
in this unbearable archaeology.

How quickly the planet can take itself back. I saw this
once in the summer in daylight, corn dangling bronze, flat
farm land growing flatter, eaten up in highways, tonight,
big and rolling it is storming in its sleep. A cop is standing at its
lip

Coca-cola can light, the car shakes, trembles along as in a
gutter, a bellow of wind rushes into my face breathless
checking the snowbank, I might have seen something
out there, every two minutes the imagination conjures
an exact bridge, the mind insists on solidity, we lose
the light of the car ahead, in the jagged beam of the cop's
blistering eye we lose the names of things, the three of us,
two women who love women, one man with so many demons
already his left foot is cold, still, making our way to Chatham,
Buxton, waiting as they once waited for Black travellers like us,
blanketed, tracked in this cold shimmering.

Out there I see nothing . . . not one thing out there
just the indifference of a cop. It takes us six hours
to travel three. I coil myself up into a nerve and quarrel
with the woman, lover, and the man for landing me in
this white hell.

We have been in this icy science only a short time. What
we are doing here is not immediately understandable
and no one is more aware of it than we, she from Uganda
via Kenya running from arranged marriages, he from Sri
Lanka via Colombo English-style boarding school to make him
the minister of the interior, me hunting for slave castles with a
pencil for explosives, what did we know that our pan-colonial
flights would end up among people who ask stupid questions
like, where are you from . . . and now here we are on their road,
in their snow, faced with their childishness.

How are we to say that these paths are involuntary and
the line of trees we are looking for will exist when we
find it, that this snow is just a cipher for our feverishness.

Only Sarah Vaughan thank god sings in this snow, Sarah
and her big band . . . gotta right to sing the blues . . .
I desert the others to her voice, fanning fire, then, even Sarah
cannot take me away but she moves the car and we live
on whatever she's given to this song, each dive of her voice,
each swoop, her vibrato holds us to the road, the outcome
of this white ride depends on Sarah's entries and exits from a
note. We cannot turn back, ahead Buxton must hear this so we
can arrive, up ahead Sarah singing she can see the midnight sun.

Only this much sound, only this much breath, only this much
grace, only how long, only how much road can take us away.

That cop's face has it. "They had been in this vast and dark
country only a short time."* Something there, written as
wilderness, wood, nickel, water, coal, rock, prairie, erased
as Athabasca, Algonquin, Salish, Inuit . . . hooded in Buxton
fugitive, Preston Black Loyalist, railroaded to gold mountain,
swimming in *Komagata Maru* . . . Are we still moving?
Each body submerged in its awful history. When will we arrive?
In a motel room later, we laugh, lie that we are not harmed,
play poker and fall asleep, he on the floor with his demons,
she, legs wrapped around me.

How can we say that when we sign our names in letters
home no one can read them, when we send photographs
they vanish. Black heart, blackheart . . . can't take it tonight
across this old road . . . take me home some other way.

* from Joseph Conrad's "An Outpost of Progress"

THROUGH MY IMPERFECT MOUTH
AND LIFE AND WAY

XIV i

I know you don't like poems, especially mine
and especially since mine never get told when
you need them, and I know that I live some
inner life that thinks it's living outside but
isn't and only wakes up when something knocks
too hard and when something is gone as if gazing
up the road I miss the bus and wave a poem at
its shadow. But bus and shadow exist all the same
and I'll send you more poems even if they arrive
late. What stops us from meeting at this place
and imagining ourselves big as the world and broad
enough to take it in and grow ancient is fear and
our carelessness, and standing in the thrall
of the wicked place we live in and not seeing
a way out all the time and never clearly all at once
and not at the same time and abandoning each other
to chance and small decisions, but if I ever thought
that I could never recover the thought struggling
to live through my imperfect mouth and life and way,
if I thought that I could do nothing about the world
then . . . well, and we've hung on to old hurts as if
that was all there was and as if no amount of sadness
would be enough for our old, insistent,
not becoming selves; and as if sadness should not end,
so for this I'll send you more poems even if they
only wave and even if I only look up late to see
your shadow rushing by.

XIV ii
to be passed on to Teresa when thinking

And no I did not know you, who could? choosing
once as you did to live in the middle of race
and not knowing the trouble of it, or perhaps
stunned by it once you did, no you may have
toyed with the idea for a moment that you were
dangerous or then harmless and that no one was
looking or everyone, and that you of all could
bound the leap of it, or perhaps not so self
possessed at all you grabbed what joy there was
you white, he black, and dangerous again,
dangerous lived some possibility until the cold
kick of self hatred found the centre of you.
I met you and avoided you at the same time
and I know the pain you wrought in a daughter, know
it holds her sometimes and heaves her and I've sat
at the kitchen table watching her forgive you everything
and telling her don't be so generous, save something
for herself because I know people just live their lives
sometimes, feeling harm is just part of the deal
and they'll give it as much as take it and how people
grow calluses to seal up wounds as you sewed
challenge in your voice to pace your stutters
and your stutters in their turn hesitated over some
childhood damage; how your face became opaque
and swollen from placing your daughters in harm's way,
how you went far away across a country to forget
but your face remained as still, how neither of them
could run from that or keep it and in fits and starts try
to recover from your rage and love; what I wanted
to say, and did, the morning you died was "Well, Teresa,
you gone, then go, and I don't know what saying go
peacefully means here, but go however you can.
Whatever's unfinished will stay and perhaps

we cannot hope to finish anything, which is life's
harsh caution, and why we must work to be gentle
here. Anyway, go how you can." Unfinished
is how you joked one morning at the kitchen sink
in Toronto after I avoided you the night before
about who deserves the world and who works hard,
". . . And another thing you!" you said laughing,
and I, "oh no, don't start with me again!" but that
was the truce and your admission that sometimes
you saw yourself honestly. But yourself and what
you had to answer for was too hard to take truthfully
so you spoke the easy version, the one they give us
and condemn us to repeat, condemning ourselves
in our own mouths. No, I did not know you, nor love,
and did not need to, to glimpse and glimpse recognition
in your face when you heard the name, Sparrow. That
is all I know, and how you pace over a daughter's face
waiting to go.

I had hoped that she could see me, hoped
that she noticed that I think these things and
furiously even if I look like some stone sitting
there hoping that I turn to stone, my own life,
from where, terrifying me and my instincts saying
don't move; we assume we know the thoughts of
those we make come close, or we forget we don't
and need not. I could make no assumptions with her,
no certainties, and at first that was the charm,
after all what was certainty before then but grief
and this looked like the opposite. But my guesses
were bad and hers too because a stone does not
have legs and arms and is only thinking of its
stoniness and wants to draw everything into its gravity
and becomes confused with flight and uncertainty,
and air wanders off to its own airiness, and becomes
impatient, eager to find more space and more music
and more intelligence, unless they are willing to
see more than themselves in each other, then
stone and air it is, fighting about their most
finite and unchangeable territories and not seeing
the sign they make defining each other.
I had hoped that she would come to see my stillness
as not mere stillness but trying to hang on and
make some steady motion in a life too busy with my
family's nervousness and I know this word "hoped,"
I mistake for done, and sitting affecting stone may
look like nothing but it is hard and all I could do
to hold myself. There are rooms across this city full
of my weeping, rooms I've woken up in at three or
four in the morning and felt only loss and distance;
there are rooms I'm ashamed to revisit full
of my worst moments, foreign and hard, rooms that felt
to me like hell. I didn't come to anything easy, not food,

not knowledge, not hands, not the skin on my back,
nothing smooth and if it was up to life my feet would be
bare and cracked and walking the hot pitched road at Guaya
with a broken face and hungry or tonight I would be
sitting ghostlike in a doorway in lamplight, my fingers
in smoke and my head tied in the violence of some man.
No one leaves that easy and I don't forget it and
it can always grip me and everything must measure this
and it's like someone escaping that I run to mere breathing.

EVERY CHAPTER OF THE WORLD

XV

today then, her head is thudding
as wet sand and as leaden,

today is the day after, rum soaked,
she went to bed deciding what she wasn't,

didn't she used to be that girl
her skirt razor pleated, her blouse hot iron blown,

who never leaned back, who was walking home
books in hand, the red primers blooding

over her palms, knowing nothing,
knowing no one alive inside her after

knowing nothing
nothing more

she should have stopped and changed shape
conch or mantis,

anyway
prayed

against the concrete wall, bitten the chain-link fencing,
prayed not to turn corners, not to enter any streets,

the moment she sees anything life is over,
she should have memorised the town better

so she would not vanish from it like the hill,
and should have memorised the hill so she wouldn't

notice herself noticing everything
like someone planning to leave

stopped then, and changed shape,
perhaps a woman rounding in uterus

clamping her teeth shut on cloth,
she watches a jar with water and lilies

unable to drink much more,
look one drop sweated from each head,

then is a woman turning inward
only flesh waiting to fall

her head is full of arrows
her head is chained to flight instead,

she's fingering blued pebbles, charred stories swirling in her way,
she's lost the kind of knowledge that makes you last

tells you how to change your shape and only
halfway in everything, halfway shapeless, halfway

different, she should have steered clear of
paper's fragrance, her head is heaving boulders

today she went to bed in a bundle of water
trembling, her teeth tasting the varnish

on the banister, in dim light, the verandah humid,
laughing into a joke and the shadow of the soursop tree

shedding scent and the street lamp will do
in the street's darkness, the distemper wash rubbing off

on the back of her feet, her calves, chalked,
it's the sodden world, only worse,

she had innocence before, shivering but innocence,
even if the banister shivers too, the rent twelve

dollars short each month, her hands embrace
damp, her middle thin like a leaf, and all on

the verandah laughing into a shape she'll
peel off and multiply until rum soaked she

will not recognise this, she will not be able
to go back with any assurances that this is

what she saw, it rains in every single
room, her throat thick with her tongue and

prayers that don't work because she won't believe
anyone can fix the dread her eyes bleed, she'll

leave this earth in water, in rust, in the
stink of its breath, in whose mouth she shrivels,

a gecko travels an earthen wall and
someone watches, the gecko is unordinary

the watcher unordinary, the wall determined, unordinary
the watchful wall, the stringy forefeet, the veined eyes

she is struck by the evenness of this proposition
sitting just so, this minute could last always

if she goes outside it will be the same
the wall, the gecko, the watcher, the even

wall, the even gecko, the even watcher, no
movement on her part will change it and the

light outside will melt all into more evenness,
it will bank off the wall, the someone, and the stringed

forefeet, the forefeet with no ending, beginning
in the grainy thick of the gecko's belly, it will be something

like twilight, lemon, like something she licks off
her fingers, and powdery, the gecko's string something

like an open conclusion, all even, the gecko says,
what the horizon does to the eyes, smoothing

precipices, summing up the small matter of
the spectrum in lemon light, blanket,

shadow, daubed oven; what if we left the earth
ajar like this?

she stands in this wrapping of the gecko and the wall,
her head shaking, still, murmuring pain,

nothing glorious about the world,
nothing coming soon, all that moment, thin dress limp,

lingering on the Morris chair, caught in the gate, torn,
and all that found in drizzling rain,

the mouth of the world will open
yawn her in, float her like a language on its tongue,

forgetting
all at once and therefore unfading surprise

at the hard matter of vanity, the relentless conceit
of hatred, surprise, thinking a warm evening

a reasoning gecko in twilight, lemon, a girl's dress
caught in a gate; it can never measure the length of this

tongue of conquest, language of defeat, she's
heard everything before, and would gladly drizzle

into the gecko's string and wall and licked evening,
if she could slip her head, so used to the mind's

enervating sleep on this whole chain of centuries,
she knows every chapter of the world describes

a woman draped in black and blood, in white
and powder, a woman crippled in dancing and

draped in dictators' dreams, in derelicts' hearts,
in miners' lights, in singers' shoes, in statues,

in all nouns' masculinities, in rocks cut out in
every single jungle and desert secret carried

in water's murmur, claps of civilisation, in poets
and workmen on the Panama Canal, all bridges,

barrios, tunnels called history, a woman gutted
and hung in prayer, run on with fingers, sacredly

stitched, called history and victory and government
halls, simmered in the residue of men crying vinegar,

every chapter of the world describes a woman at her own
massacre, carvings of her belly, blood gouache blood

of her face, hacked in revolutions of the sun and kitchens,
gardens of her eyes, asphalt lakes, in telescopes and bureau

drawers, in paper classifieds, telephones, exalted memories,
declarations, a woman at her funeral arrangements, why

perhaps so much of literature enters her like entering
a coffin, so much props up a ragged corpse she thinks,

the dry thin whistle of its mouth, the dead clatter
of its ribs, the rain in its room all day, all night, all

evening, the women walking out of its skull one
by one by one, if she lowers her eyes everything falls

out, if she lowers her eyes from this then perhaps
the rattling gecko could have its say, instead

suspicious, she asks, what gender, as if what
guarantee, if not certainty, how does she hold

a head full of curses, all her days are cracked
in half and crumble,

she can't think of it that way, all tidy like a swept floor
the broom resting out of sight and the unsightly

swept, she can't think of it that way, as just
doings of a passing race, so many clouds of ants

so many fields of fish, and later reassembling
in another tragedy of metal and chemical winds,

so no matter. You see, to circle enemies and
greet them like metropolitan politicians do

is the liberal way, to circle, accept, so
much southern death is a sign of talent

No she cannot speak of this or that massacre, this
or that war like a poet. Someone else will do that. She

sees who dies. Someone with not a hope but a photograph
of someone they loved, walking an Azerbaijan street, a man

and a boy and grief covering their mouth like a handkerchief,
and that feeling in the belly of all gone.

Someone moaning the name of a country, this country, in
Belet Huen, flesh melting into his blood,

in the pulp of human flesh he becomes, blindfolded
and longing for a gateway, a fence, a way out, the way in

which led him by the belly. Someone crawling
at a game of soldiers with a dog's chain and in urine,

"I love the KKK" written on his back and his white comrades
braying and kicking, someone who

the next morning will confess to his skin
and all tribunals saying, no, no, I did not feel that. It was not

race.
Someone scrubbing a plastic tablecloth

in Regent Park saying, "I have talked to God
and he knows, I hope, that I am here."

Scrubbing the plastic flowers off the plastic tablecloth
hoping that god is listening.

Someone whose face you cannot see nor want to, her
dress around her fashionable and stiff with

blood, bent over, as if making a bed on a pavement,
smoothing out a corner of the sheet, she drowns

in the openings of her heart.
Someone in the tumbled rush of bodies cutting out

her own singular life
and the life of a child running with her to a refugee

camp on the Burundi border, caught
in the bulb of a television camera, seen

in her most private moment,
tumbling to the bottom of a mass grave after all her running.

"Assuming we speak of the civilised
world – reflecting a belief in diversity, peace,

economic liberalism and democracy – the choice
is obvious." When editorials dust themselves clean

she dreams noise wrapping the door, disappearing
gunboats steaming toward the middle of America,

bananas floating in the creamy eyes of business
men, old instruction books on the care and discipline

of slaves, not to go too far back, after all not
their fault, no need, plenty enough current

destruction, but then what are we assuming,
left unsaid, if undone, to repeat, Guatemala,

Nicaragua, Dominican Republic, Haiti, Grenada, Costa
Rica, Colombia, Chile, Mexico, all other anagrams scuttling

off that page, inventory is useless now but just to say
not so fast, not so clever, boy, circumnavigating

parentheses may be easy but not the world,
the uncivilised at the end of the day in trucks' dust clouds,

at water holes on the edges of deserts, at moonlight
waiting for crabs to march on beaches, settling into

a doorway's shawl, thinking at last a cup of water, thinking
the blanket stuck around the window will keep the rawness

out, thinking of shoe factory jobs, button factory jobs,
thread, at lines for work, at zones metamorphosing at

borders, moving as if in one skin to camps, smelling
oil wells, sugar burning, cathode smoke, earth drained

of water, earth flooded with water, rivers of slick,
overloaded ferries, all belongings bursting in suitcases

and bundles at more borders, starving in the arms
of offshore democrats with Miami bank accounts,

the tired voting in surrender, those left after the war,
those left after the peace, both feel the same, war or peace,

surrender then if it means powdered milk, if it means
rice, semolina, surrender for airflights out of barren

ice, barren water, barren villages, surrender all parentheses,
all arguments, this world in that one, that one in this

all tangled, the revolutions of an engine turning up refugees,
corporate boards, running shoes, new economic plans

but surrender the parentheses, what are those
but tongues slipping in and out of a mouth, pages

sounding like wings beating in air, what but the sound
of someone washing their hands quickly, beating their lips red.

She looks and she surrenders too, she
surrenders leaning into the moonlight on the verandah,

she surrenders her thoughts and circumnavigations
of her skull to rum, when they ask what became of her,

what was her trouble, no lover, childhood beatings,
loneliness, a weakness for simple dichotomies, poor, rich

black
white

female
male

well if it must be said their details too, and
their missions, wandering through us like a sickness.

She may not leave here anything but a prisoner
circling a cell,

cutting the square smaller and smaller and walking into herself
finally, brushing against herself as against surprising

flesh in a dark room. She
hears the *shsh* of cloth, the friction of her hands.

Even if she goes outside the cracks in her throat will break
as slate, her legs still cutting the cell in circles.

ACKNOWLEDGEMENTS

I would like to thank Ted Chamberlin for his ongoing support, his friendship, and his editorial acuity.

Thanks also to Adrienne Rich and Michael Ondaatje, who read early drafts of the book.